When Parents Separate

Pete Sanders and Steve Myers

Aladdin / Watts
London • Sydney

© Aladdin Books Ltd 2004

Designed and produced by
Aladdin Books Ltd
28 Percy Street
London W1T 2BZ

New edition
first published in
Great Britain in 2004 by
Franklin Watts
96 Leonard Street
London EC2A 4XD

ISBN 0 7496 5403 1

Original edition published as
What Do You Know About –
Divorce and Separation

A catalogue record for this
book is available from the
British Library.

Printed in UAE
Editor
Harriet Brown

Designers
Flick, Book Design & Graphics
Simon Morse

Illustrator
Mike Lacey

Picture Research
Brian Hunter Smart

CONTENTS

How to use this book

The books in this series deal with issues that
may affect the lives of many young people.

- Each book can be read by a young person
  alone, or together with an adult.

- Issues raised in the storyline are further
  discussed in accompanying text.

- A list of practical ideas is given in the 'What
  can we do?' section at the end of the book.

- Organisations and helplines are listed for
  additional information and support.

INTRODUCTION

" Today, separation and divorce are widely considered to be acceptable choices for people who are no longer happy in their relationship. "

An increasing number of young people may, at some point in their lives, have to deal with the divorce or separation of parents or other close relatives.

This book explains what divorce and separation mean, and looks at some of the reasons why relationships come to an end.

It considers the effects that separation and divorce can have on people's lives. Each chapter introduces a different aspect of the subject, illustrated by a continuing storyline. The characters in the story face situations and feelings that many people will experience. After each episode, we look at some of the issues raised, and widen out the discussion. By the end, you will understand more about how divorce and separation can affect families, and the emotions that might have to be faced.

I have a friend at school whose parents split up, but now they're together again.

My mum says people shouldn't divorce if there are children involved. Maybe that's the reason.

Well, my parents couldn't divorce if they wanted to. It's against our religion.

RELATIONSHIPS

> For many people, relationships make a huge difference to the quality of their lives. Sharing experiences with other people can add to our own enjoyment of them.

At some point in their lives, many adults will form an intimate and long-term relationship with another person.

Couples might declare their commitment to each other by getting married. Or they may live together without being married. The decision will depend on the people involved and their own attitudes and beliefs. For most people, getting to know someone very well before beginning this kind of partnership is of great importance. How a relationship begins can affect the way it develops. Rushing into things can create possible problems later on. For example, people's attitudes, values and interests often change as time goes by, and this can put a strain on even the closest of relationships. Although there are ups and downs in any relationship, it is important to remember that sometimes they do end, even though we might not want them to.

In our lives, we are involved in many relationships with other people. Some may be casual acquaintances; others become good friends. There are many sorts of relationships. Good relationships and friendships can add to our own sense of well-being.

One day after school...

... Daniel Sharp asked his friend Josh Tyler if he wanted to play football in the park.

After the film, Josh offered to buy Emily a hamburger.

Josh took Emily home and walked the short distance to his house.

Josh told his gran about Emily's parents not being married.

The whole family was waiting for him. His older sister, Sarah, had brought her boyfriend, Raj, round.

Josh's younger sister, Lauren, ran out of the room, crying. Everyone was suddenly silent.

It's horrible at home. Mum and Dad argue so much. They wouldn't notice if I wasn't there.

Josh is worried because his parents argue all the time. Arguments can occur in any relationship. For some people, arguments are a way of expressing how they feel. Hearing your parents argue can be upsetting. They might not realise the effect it has on you. However, this does not necessarily mean they love each other any less.

Why are you splitting up? It can't be true. I won't let it be true!

Relationships do not always stay the same.
Accepting that relationships change can be hard, because it means acknowledging that you will not always be as close to some people as you once were. For instance, the arrival of a new baby may mean some changes for everyone in the family. Or, it may be that, as you grow to know a person better, your feelings towards that person change.

Marriage and society
Marriage is an expression of the way two people feel about each other. It confirms a life-long commitment to each other.

• Many couples don't marry, even though they may live and have children together.

• Choosing whether or not to marry need not affect two people's commitment to, and love for, each other and their children.

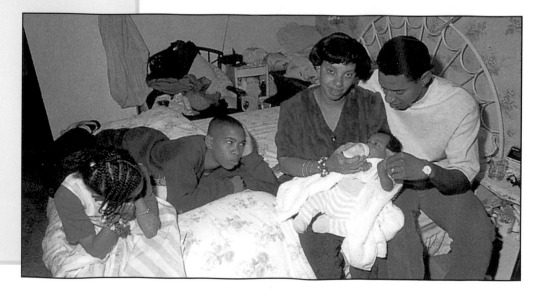

SEPARATION AND DIVORCE

> A couple who are no longer happy in their relationship may decide to separate. If they are married, they may also decide to divorce.

Divorce is the legal end of a marriage. Until a divorce is confirmed, a couple remain married in the eyes of the law, whether or not they live together. A separation may also involve some legal issues.

Some people see divorce as a more significant step than separation, because it brings an official end to a relationship. But whether or not two people are married, the process of separation and divorce is rarely easy for anyone involved. For young people, the breakdown of their parents' relationship may raise strong emotions. It can often seem as though their own feelings are not being considered. When an intimate relationship between two adults ends, they will no longer have a say in each other's life. A child might only live with one parent on a regular basis, but both parents may continue to share the responsibilty of caring.

When a parent decides to live apart from his or her partner and children, it raises difficult feelings for everyone involved, including the adults who have made the decision to separate.

7

Half an hour later...

... Josh was sitting on the sofa, talking to his mother. Sarah and Raj had left.

> Why didn't you tell me before? You've obviously told Sarah.

> We should have done, Josh. I'm sorry. We didn't want to hurt you – or Lauren.

> Well you have, haven't you? But when have you worried about how we feel?

> That's not fair, Josh. You know your dad and I both love you. This isn't the end of the world. Things will still be the same.

Mr Tyler came into the room. He had been upstairs talking to Lauren.

> Don't say that, dear. It isn't true. And it won't make it any easier for Josh and Lauren.

> She's calmer now, but she's still crying. I've put her to bed. She won't fall asleep for a bit.

> Are you going to get a divorce?

> Perhaps. We're going to separate for a while first.

Josh said he felt tired, and didn't want to talk about it any more that night. He went up to Lauren's room.

> Why is this happening, Josh? I don't understand. I don't like Mum and Dad fighting, but I want them both to be here.

> I know, Lauren. So do I. This is awful. Everything's going to change.

Josh didn't sleep well that night. The next day, Daniel noticed something was wrong.

> What happened? Did you and the lovely Emily split up?

> Not now, Daniel. I'm not in the mood for jokes.

Daniel realised something was seriously wrong. Eventually, Josh decided to tell Daniel the truth.

Josh hadn't realised that Daniel's dad was actually his stepfather.

The same thing happened to me, but I was younger. I don't remember much, but the atmosphere at home was terrible. Things got better after they split.

But how can things be better? They won't be together.

Maybe they won't get divorced. Mum just said they're separating.

You're always going on about how much they argue. My parents were always arguing. They don't anymore. They're friends. Dad even gets on with my stepdad.

At home that evening, Lauren talked to her gran.

School was horrible today, Gran. I felt like people were staring at me. I daren't tell anyone about Mum and Dad.

I don't think they'd be as shocked as you imagine.

You don't understand. Most of them go on about how great their parents are.

I don't understand. I don't like Mum and Dad fighting, but I want them both to be here.

Finding out that your parents are separating can cause great distress. This can be worse if you are not told the truth, or hear about it by accident, as Josh and Lauren have done. Parents may be unsure how to tell their children about their decision. They may give different versions of the situation which makes it more difficult to understand.

The atmosphere at home used to be terrible. Things got better after Mum and Dad separated.

Some couples have a 'trial separation'. They separate for a while to sort out how they feel about each other. They may decide to try again, or they may realise that they are better off apart and decide to separate permanently.

Many people who have separated remain friends, despite not wanting to be a couple any more. If two people have realised that they no longer love each other, or that their being together is only causing them and those around them distress, they may decide that breaking up is the most sensible solution. If the break-up itself is without a great deal of conflict, it can be easier to adjust to the new situation. However, most separations are likely to create unhappy feelings and take some getting used to.

WHY DO RELATIONSHIPS BREAK DOWN?

> " Relationships end for many reasons. The causes may be similar but each situation will be different. "

The decision to separate or divorce may be made because of one specific action or might be the result of a build-up of circumstances.

Some couples grow apart naturally, as their interests change. They may discover they no longer have very much in common. Not everyone has the same expectations of a relationship, and this might not become apparent until people have been living together for a while. Sometimes people enter a relationship believing they will be able to change aspects of their partner's behaviour or attitude which they don't like. Physical or emotional abuse may be a factor in some break-ups. Others might seek sexual relationships with different people. This can make their partner feel jealous or betrayed. It is important to remember that the situations described above do not necessarily mean that a couple will separate. Relationships that work well are the ones in which people can talk openly, and discuss any problems and concerns they may have.

Just as friends have arguments, so too do adults in a close relationship. Often the problems can be sorted out, but sometimes the nature of the relationship needs to change.

The following weekend...

... Mr Tyler moved out of the house.

I wish you didn't have to go, Dad.

Don't worry, princess, I'm not far away. You can call me whenever you like.

A couple of weeks later...

... Sarah and Raj came round. Mrs Tyler had not yet arrived home from work.

So, how are things?

Ok, I suppose. Dad came round to see us the other night.

He and Mum started arguing, as usual.

Things were still no better between Mr and Mrs Tyler.

Your mum and dad never talk to each other. They just shout. In my day you worked together to put things right. It's too easy to give up these days.

That's what my father says, too.

He says that because it's easier to get a divorce, people are more likely to do it.

In your day, Gran, there were lots of unhappy couples that were afraid to divorce because of what society would think. It's not such a big deal today, but it's still painful.

I need to ask you something, Mum. I don't really know how to say it.

You can ask me anything, you know that.

The next day, Josh talked to his mum alone.

Neither of them saw Lauren come into the kitchen.

Have you or Dad met someone else? Is that why you're separating?

No, darling. It's nothing like that, I promise.

People do separate because they meet someone else. But that's not what happened with us. Maybe your gran's right. She thought we married too young. We didn't want our marriage to fail, but sometimes these things happen.

That evening, Josh found Lauren crying in the garden. He asked her what the matter was.

It's all my fault. I'm the reason Dad's gone.

Don't be silly! Why would you think that?

I took some money from Dad last week, without telling him. I'm being paid back for doing wrong, like Gran always says.

A few days later...

... Josh and Emily went to the pictures. He told her what Lauren had said.

I heard you talking to Mum. She said they didn't want to break up. It must be because of what I've done.

I'm sure it's not like that.

I know Lauren's story can't be true. But I wonder if it isn't partly our fault. Mum and Dad do argue about us. Maybe if we'd acted differently things would be ok.

Josh, you're not to blame for what your parents do. Come on, forget about it for a while. Let's enjoy the film.

> I wonder if it isn't partly our fault. Mum and Dad do argue about us.

Josh has convinced himself that his parents' separation is his fault.
If young people can't understand the reason for their parents' decision to split up, they may assume that they are to blame. But young people are not responsible for the behaviour of their mum and dad. Talking openly and calmly with your parents, siblings and friends can help you to understand the situation.

Reasons for breaking up
Reasons for a break-up can be complicated.

- Often, only the people who are in the relationship are fully aware of the circumstances.

- If a relationship is based on false hopes, it is less likely to survive than one based on trust and open communication.

> In my day you worked together to put things right. It's too easy to give up these days.

Gran believes that today it is too easy to divorce.
It used to be much harder to get a divorce; it was only allowed under special circumstances. Some people, like Gran, think that couples will be tempted to divorce instead of working at a relationship. This may be true in some cases, but for many divorce is a last resort. Lots of marriages are able to overcome problems.

14

TAKING SIDES

" It is natural for young people to have mixed loyalties when their parents separate and to feel torn between the two parents. "

Children can come under a lot of pressure to support one parent against another. This is particularly true if people who are breaking up feel hostile towards one another.

Some children have a 'favourite' parent. Or they might prefer being with Mum for one activity and with Dad for another. Feeling you have to choose one over another can be confusing and hurtful. Adults sometimes forget that children have the right to be supportive of both parents, without feeling disloyal. This is especially true when other members of the family are voicing their opinions and laying blame. Everyone might appear to have a different point of view and it can seem impossible to decide what the truth is. Each person involved will have their own understanding of the situation. It is your right to form your own opinions and you shouldn't feel disloyal about doing so.

Young people may sometimes feel torn between their parents. But it can also be painful for a parent to come to terms with the fact that his or her child will continue to love and support the other parent.

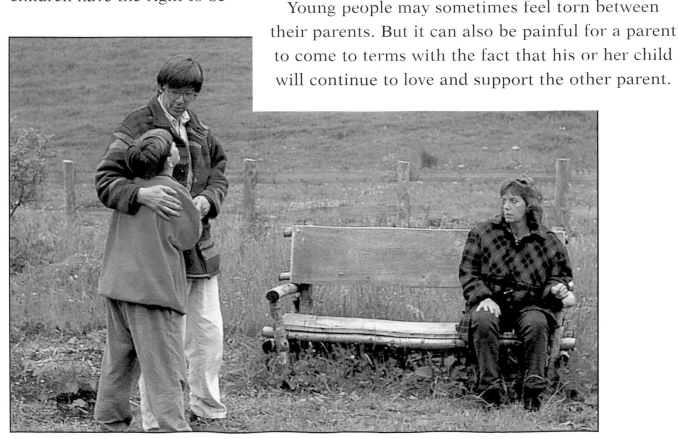

A few months later...

... Lauren came home just as her mum was slamming the telephone receiver down.

Lauren ran up to her room. Later, her mum tried to talk to her.

The following weekend was Josh's birthday. His mum arranged a small party for him.

His mum walked away. Josh turned to Lauren.

Mr Tyler arrived a little while later with Josh's present. He'd bought him the football strip.

After his dad left, Josh danced with Emily. He said his mum was upset.

> She said Dad's trying to buy our loyalty. I don't know what to believe anymore.

You may hear different versions of what is going on.
Making sense of a situation like this is never easy. Hearing people say nasty things about someone you love is also upsetting. Your feelings for your parents don't have to change just because their feelings for each other have.

Mr Tyler has bought presents for Josh and Lauren.
A separated parent might feel the need to provide treats for the children. This can be because he or she wants to show the children how much they are loved or to make up for any unhappiness that has been caused. It can make you feel special, but it can also be difficult for the other parent, particularly if he or she is not in a position to do the same.

> I don't know what I saw in your dad. I'm glad none of you take after him.

Sometimes adults let out their angry feelings about each other to their children.
After a divorce or separation, adults often feel unsure of themselves and their position with their children. They may ask their children which parent they love most. They are probably doing this because of their own confusion, but it only makes the situation harder for young people. You may think that whatever you say or do will be wrong, because you will be betraying one parent by agreeing with the other. It is best to be honest about how you feel.

ATTITUDES TO DIVORCE

> Although separation and divorce are more accepted nowadays, there are those who still hold strong views about the subject.

For many people, marriage is for life, and divorce is not an option. This could be because of their religious or cultural beliefs.

Some people believe that couples should stay together, no matter what difficulties arise. Others disagree. They see no reason, for instance, why a person who is being mistreated within a marriage or other close relationship should have to put up with it. Another view is that divorce should be allowed, provided that there are no children involved. On the other hand, young people who are miserable because their parents are always arguing or obviously no longer love each other, may feel a sense of relief when the decision to separate is made.

The reality is that there are no easy answers. In each case, it is up to the people within the relationship to try to decide what is best for them.

Some religions and cultures believe that divorce is never acceptable. Some marriage services stress that, no matter what, the couple's commitment is to each other, and is for life.

The following month...

It was the start of the school holidays. Emily invited some friends round to her house one afternoon.

How come your parents get on so well, and mine can't stand being in the same room?

Don't worry, Josh. Mum and Dad will get back together.

How can you be so sure?

I have a friend at school whose parents split up, but now they're together again.

My mum says people shouldn't divorce if there are children involved.

My parents couldn't divorce if they wanted to. It's against our religion.

Everyone started to talk about marriage and relationships.

I was really worried about telling my friends that Mum and Dad weren't living together anymore. I thought they'd make fun of me.

Some people might. Most know it's nothing to be ashamed of.

I felt the same about discussing my stepdad. Then I found out that quite a few of my friends' parents have divorced or remarried.

The next day...

... Mr Tyler came round to the house. He and Mrs Tyler had some news.

You know we've been living apart for months now.

Your dad and I have been discussing what we should do. We both think it's for the best for us to get a divorce.

You can't! It isn't fair.

You both know things haven't been any easier since we split up.

We never promised you that we would get back together, darling. We did try.

Maybe you haven't tried hard enough.

Maybe you just need more time.

I'm sorry. We know this is hard for you. But it just wouldn't work.

You lied to us! You said you were just going to separate for a while.

Mr and Mrs Tyler talked to Josh and Lauren for a while. Everyone was very upset.

I was worried about telling my friends that Mum and Dad weren't living together anymore.

Some young people are ashamed to admit that their parents are separating. But as Josh has discovered, lots of his friends have been through the same thing. It is normal to experience all kinds of emotions during your parents' divorce. Talking to people whose parents are separated or divorced will help you realise you're not alone and that, with time, things should get easier.

Lauren is certain that her mum and dad will get back together again. Some young people hold on to the belief that their parents will eventually decide that they do want to be together. However upsetting it is, refusing to admit the relationship is beyond repair will not help you to deal with the situation.

Don't worry about it, Josh. I'm sure Mum and Dad will get back together.

My mum says people shouldn't divorce if children are involved.

Some people believe that a couple should stay together if they have children, whatever difficulties they may have. The upheaval of their parents' separation can be hard on young people. But in some cases, living with parents who are unhappy with each other may present just as many problems.

THE DIVORCE PROCESS

" Any couple is able to separate without taking legal action. A divorce, however, is a legal process. "

The rules for granting a divorce vary from country to country. In most cases, the decision will depend on certain factors.

There are many reasons why people apply for a divorce and why a divorce is granted. It may be because of mental cruelty, or physical abuse from their partner. Or it might be that a person has had a sexual relationship outside the marriage. Divorce is usually allowed if two people have lived apart for a certain period of time. In many situations, both partners have agreed that divorce is the best choice. Sometimes, they may have serious disagreements about various points. These are often to do with financial matters and each person's role in bringing up children from the relationship. In these cases, it can take a long time for people to sort out the details, and in the end the courts may have to decide. The law can require one adult to give up a proportion of his or her earnings to support the other partner or any children involved.

In some countries, the law requires couples who want to divorce to undergo counselling. This is to make sure they have thought carefully about the situation and are sure that divorce is the best resolution.

One afternoon soon afterwards...

... Sarah and Raj came round. Mr and Mrs Tyler had gone to see their solicitor.

Why do they need a solicitor?

Divorce is a legal process. They need someone who can help them with all the details.

Such as what?

Because Mum and Dad own the house together, but aren't going to be married anymore, they have to decide how to divide the property.

They also have to make arrangements to make sure your dad gives your mum enough money to look after you.

They explained about the decisions that would have to be made.

Dad told us it's easier if we live here with Mum. They didn't ask how we felt about it.

It feels like we're being left out of everything. All the decisions are being made about what's going to happen and we find out afterwards. It's not fair.

But things are sometimes worse than this. I remember when my friend's parents divorced. It was terrible. They fought over everything. They had to sell the house. They couldn't agree about who the children should live with. The courts had to decide in the end.

Josh said it was different for Sarah, because she didn't live there any more.

Sarah said that divorces can go on for a long time.

I just wish Mum and Dad would talk to us more and explain what's going on.

I know it's hard. It's hard for me too.

Don't forget they're going through a lot too, Lauren. There's a lot to sort out.

Sometimes people get so caught up in everything that they forget about other things that matter just as much. You have to be patient.

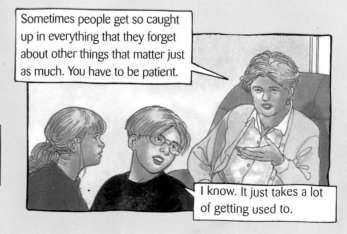

I know. It just takes a lot of getting used to.

Because Mum and Dad own the house together, they have to decide how to divide the property.

When a couple lives together, most of the things they own often belong to both of them. If they break up, they will need to make arrangements, as Josh and Lauren's parents are doing, to transfer ownership of their belongings to each partner separately. Sometimes there are disagreements about who gets what. Parents can forget how upsetting this can be for the children.

Most couples seek advice at some point

If the terms of a divorce are not agreed to by one of the partners, the courts may become involved.

● As well as lawyers, mediators and counsellors can help people to come to terms with their decision, and to understand what it will mean for them and their family in the future.

Dad told us it's easier if we live here with Mum. They didn't ask how we felt about it.

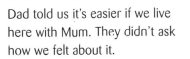

After a divorce, children will usually live for most of the time with just one parent. Which parent this should be is often the decision of the family itself. If parents can't agree, the courts may be asked to decide. The well-being of the children will be the most important factor in this. Even so, the final decision might not agree with your own understanding of what you feel is best.

EFFECTS OF DIVORCE AND SEPARATION

" A separation or divorce will usually involve some emotional upheaval for everyone concerned. "

It takes time to come to terms with the fact that your parents will no longer be together.

Although young people's reactions may differ according to their age, most will experience a range of feelings. Some young people become angry. They want to blame someone for what has happened. They might refuse to accept the situation, hoping that things will return to the way they were. Sometimes they might feel guilty, believing that they could have done something to alter the situation. A young person may feel helpless, thinking that he or she has no control over what is going on.

People's sense of self-worth can be affected by the changes at home. This might also influence their behaviour. For instance, some children refuse to go to school, or throw tantrums. Younger children may become anxious or want a lot of attention. Older children may become withdrawn or aggressive. All of these are natural reactions to a difficult and confusing situation.

It can make young people feel very lonely if they feel that younger or older brothers and sisters don't really understand what is going on.

24

A few weeks later....

... Sarah and Raj had some news of their own.

It's a shame Dad isn't here, but we thought you'd want to know. We've decided to get married.

Darling, that's wonderful news. I'm so pleased for you both.

The following evening, Emily and Josh went out again. He told her about Sarah and Raj.

I can't believe it. I think your parents have the right idea. If you don't marry, then you don't have all the hassle if things go wrong.

That's not true. It would be just as difficult for me if my parents separated.

If they ever did separate, I'd still want to get married or live with someone one day.

Emily said that was silly. He might feel like that now, but he'd change his mind when he was older.

How do you know? I'm beginning to wonder if it's all worth it.

You're not concentrating, Lauren. Is something the matter?

At school, the teacher had noticed that Lauren was not her usual self in class.

I don't want to do this. Work's stupid.

Lauren threw her book down and ran out of the classroom. That evening the teacher called Mrs Tyler in.

Lauren's a good student. She was doing well, but she's changed. She's become moody and she can be difficult to handle during lessons.

As you know, my husband and I are divorcing. I think it's hit Lauren really hard. I'll talk to her.

At home, Lauren and her mum talked.

I know you and Dad don't love each other anymore, but I still love you both. I feel like I've got to choose between you.

Oh, Lauren. You don't have to love one of us more than the other. Whatever your dad and I feel about each other, we both still love you.

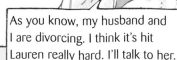

25

> I still love you both, but I feel like I've got to choose between you.

When parents split up, you may lose contact with those you care about. Young people may have to move to live with one parent. Some adults try to prevent their child from seeing the absent parent. Sometimes a child does not want to see the absent parent. It can be hurtful if one parent chooses not to see their child.

> If you don't marry, then you don't have the hassle if things go wrong.

> My husband and I are divorcing. I think it's hit Lauren really hard. I'll talk to her.

Bottling up your feelings does not make them go away. The emotions that young people have when parents separate or divorce may take some time to deal with. It might be hard to know who to speak to, especially if you think you can no longer talk to your parents, but it can help to express your feelings.

Josh's parents' divorce has made him question the value of marriage. It is natural to have these feelings, but remember that each relationship is different. Emily knows that only she and a future partner can decide what is right for them. Letting your parents' situation influence you puts barriers in the way of potentially strong relationships.

NEW BEGINNINGS

" Young people often have very little say in their
parents' decision to separate or divorce. To them,
it can seem like the end of everything. "

**In a way, it is the start of a new
period in their life. However,
recognising this means understanding
that some change is inevitable.
This is often very difficult.**

You may be told that a divorce is final.
This does not always mean that you are
ready to accept it. The emotions people
have during the break-up of a
relationship have been compared to
those of people who are grieving for
someone who has died. It can take a
long time to fully come to terms with
the situation. It is important to
consider how parents may be feeling as
well. They have been used to being part
of a couple. Adjusting to being in social
situations on their own may be
difficult. Many adults begin new
relationships. This might mean young
people becoming part of a new family
situation, and perhaps getting used to
the idea of having stepbrothers and
sisters. Seeing one parent only at set
times may seem unfair. Some young
people feel guilty because, although
they want to see their mum and dad,
the time for visits clashes with time
they would have spent with friends. If
this happens,
talking honestly
about how you feel
can help to solve
the problem.

It is not always
easy to accept that
your parents will
eventually carry
on with their lives
and may meet
new partners.

... Mr and Mrs Tyler's divorce was now final. For the first time in a long while, they were all together at Sarah and Raj's wedding.

After the ceremony, Mr Tyler spoke to Josh and Lauren.

Who's that?

That's Sheila, Dad's girlfriend. They've been going out for a while. We've only met her a couple of times, though.

She's ok, but she's trying too hard to be nice. She wants us to like her.

Don't forget – I'll pick you up next Saturday at 10:00. Have a think about what you'd like to do over the weekend.

Will Sheila be coming with us?

She could if you'd like her to. Or we can be on our own.

Bring her along if you like. She might stop you being late!

At the party afterwards, Josh noticed his Mum looking rather sad. He asked if she was ok.

I'm fine, darling, honest. It's just a big day. It's also strange to have your dad here, that's all.

Josh went to join his friends.

Was Mum ok? I saw you talking to her.

Yes. I think she's a bit upset about Dad and Sheila, but she's all right.

You both seem to be getting along better.

That's true. I told you everything would work out.

It's still odd, not having Dad around. I really miss him sometimes.

You two both seem happier about the situation now.

I know. But he and Mum both seem happier apart. We'll get used to it all, and things will go on from there.

28

That's Sheila, Dad's girlfriend. They've been going out for a while.

Like Mr Tyler, many divorced or separated people begin new relationships.
Some decide to remarry. Accepting a new person in your mum or dad's life can be hard. You may think he or she is trying to replace your other parent. Occasions where both parents are present can leave you with conflicting emotions. Feeling guilty doesn't help. Try talking openly with your parents.

Don't forget – I'll pick you up next saturday at 10:00.

Lauren and Josh only see their dad at weekends now.
Remember that although you only see your mum or dad occasionally, it doesn't mean that he or she loves you any less. Even if one or both of your parents does not seem any happier after the break-up, this does not mean that you should not feel able to enjoy yourself.

It's still odd, not having Dad around. I really miss him sometimes.

When parents separate or divorce, you may feel as though your life will never be the same again.
The break-up of a relationship can leave people feeling confused and hurt. But people adjust to new situations. With time you may realise that change can be positive. Your parents' divorce or separation means the end of a period of your life. It is also the start of another, and life will become normal again.

WHAT CAN WE DO?

" Having read this book, you will understand more about separation and divorce, and the effect they can have on everyone concerned. "

The breakdown of a relationship can be difficult for everyone involved. It can take time for everyone to adjust to the changes that are happening.

If you know someone whose parents are splitting up, or if your own parents are separating or divorcing, understanding the kinds of emotions everyone might be going through can help. It is important to remember that feeling depressed, guilty, angry or confused or looking for someone to blame are all common reactions. It is important to learn how to cope with and express these feelings. It can help to talk openly and honestly with your parents or with your friends or siblings. Although it's not easy, most people do adjust and are able to get on with their lives by accepting the new situation and taking things from there.

Adults can also help, by realising that most children want to know what is happening, and by being as honest as possible about their decisions. It is sometimes easy for adults who are divorcing or separating to forget that, just as they might be feeling upset themselves, their children may also be deeply affected.

Young people and adults who have read this book together might find it helpful to discuss how they feel about the issues raised, and to share their ideas and experiences. Anyone who would like to have more information, or to talk to someone not directly involved, may be able to obtain advice or support from the organisations listed below.

Childline
45 Folgate Street
London E1 6GL
Tel: 020 7650 3200
24-hour helpline:
0800 1111
Textphone:0800 400 222
Website: www.
childline.org.uk

The National Children's Bureau
(Promoting the interests and well-being of children)
8 Wakley Street
London EC1V 7QE
Tel: 020 7843 6000
Email: library@ncb.org.uk
Website: www.ncb.org.uk

Relate
(Relationship counselling)
Herbert Gray College
Little Church Street
Rugby CV21 3 AP
Tel: 0845 1304 010
Email: enquiries@relate.
org.uk
Website: www.relate.org.uk

The Children's Society
Edward Rudolph House
Margery Street
London WC1X 0JL
Tel: 0845 300 1128
Email: info@childrens
society.org.uk
Website: www.the-childrens-
society.org.uk

National Council for the Divorced and Separated
c/o 14 Abbots Drive
Hucknall
Nottingham
NG15 6QW
Tel: 07041 478 120
Email: nationalsecretary
@ncds.org.uk
Website: www.ncds.org.uk

Ministry of Youth
Level 5, Public Trust Building
117-125 Lambton Quay
PO Box 10-300, Wellington
New Zealand
Tel: + 64 (04) 471 2158
Email: info@
youthaffairs.govt.nz
Website: www.youthaffairs.
govt.nz

Gingerbread
7 Sovereign Close
Sovereign Court
London E1W 3HW
Tel: 0800 0184 318
Email: office@gingerbread.
org.uk
Website: www.gingerbread.
org.uk

National Family Mediation
Alexander House
Telephone Avenue
Bristol BS1 4BS
Tel: 0117 904 2825
Email: general@nfm.org.uk
Website: www.nfm.u-
net.com

National Council of Single Mothers and Their Children
ncsmc c/- Torrens Building
220 Victoria Square
Adelaide SA 5000, Australia
Tel: +61 (0) 8 8226 2505
Email: ncsmc@ncsmc.org.au
Website: www.ncsmc.org.au

INDEX

A
arguments 5, 6, 9, 11, 12, 18
ashamed, feelings of 20

B
behaviour, affected by divorce 24
blame 13, 14, 15, 24, 30
breaking up, reasons for 14
brothers and sisters 14, 15, 24

C
causes 11, 14, 21
changes in relationships 4, 6, 11
children, love for 6, 29
children, responsibility for 7, 21, 23
commitment 6, 18
contact, keeping 26
counselling 21, 23
cultural beliefs 18, 19

E
emotions, dealing with 20, 24, 26, 27, 30

F
feelings, expressing of 11, 17, 20, 24, 26, 30
financial matters 21
finding out 10
friendship 4, 11

G
getting back together 19, 20
guilt, feelings of 24, 27, 29, 30

H
honesty, need for 10, 17, 27, 29, 31

L
legal process 21, 22, 23
lifestyle changes 7, 11, 21, 23, 26, 27, 29, 30
living together 4, 6, 22
living with one parent 7, 23, 26
love 6, 8, 10, 15, 17, 18, 25, 29
loyalty to parents 15, 16, 17

M
marriage 4, 5, 6, 7, 18, 19, 25, 26
moving house 26

R
relationships 4, 6, 7, 11, 14, 18, 20, 26, 29, 30
relief, sense of 18
religious beliefs 18, 19
remarriage 20, 29

S
solicitors 23
special occasions 29
step-parent 9, 19

T
talking things through 11, 12, 17, 20, 22, 27, 29
trial separations 10
truth, different versions 10, 15, 17

W
well-being 4, 23